THIS BOOK BELONGS TO:

_____

WELCOME TO ALABAMA

Dedicated to all the explorers.

ISBN 978-1-958985-21-2

www.joeysavestheday.com

A Mimi Book

The name "Alabama" for the state was derived from the Alabama River. This river was named after the Alabama people, a Native American tribe that inhabited the region.

Alabama was the twenty-second state to join the union. It officially joined on December 14, 1890.

Alabama is situated in the Southeastern region of the United States and is bordered by four states: Mississippi, Tennessee, Georgia, and Florida.

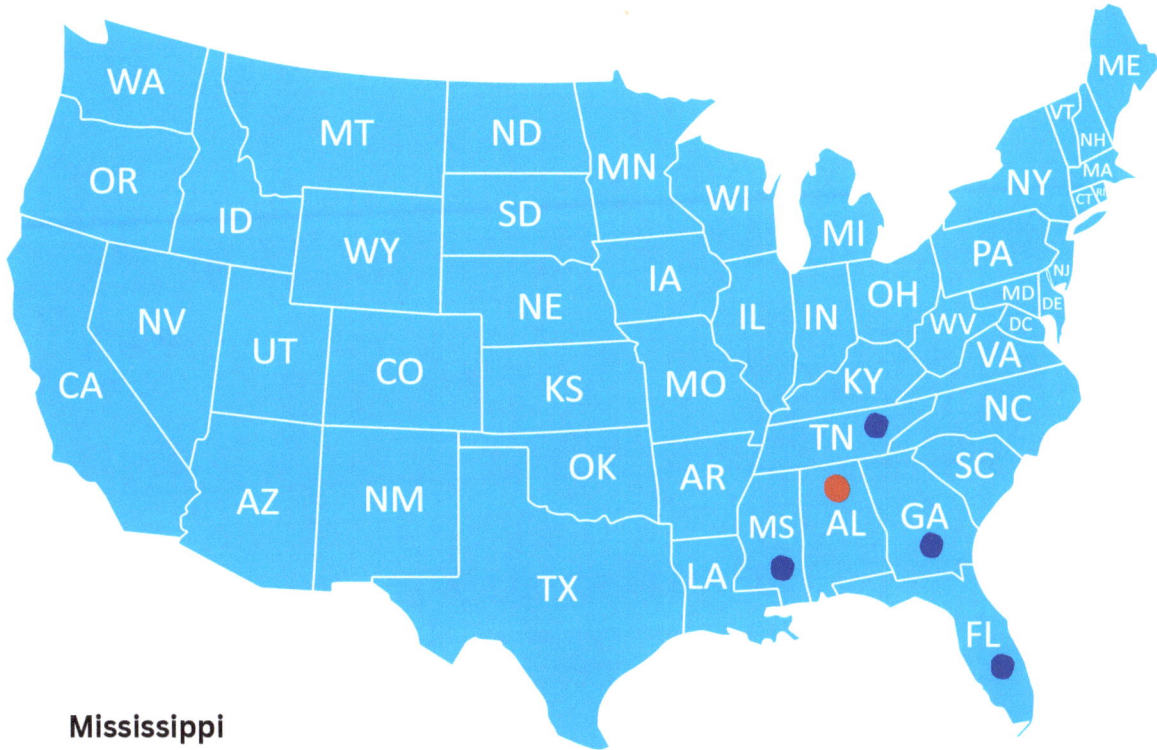

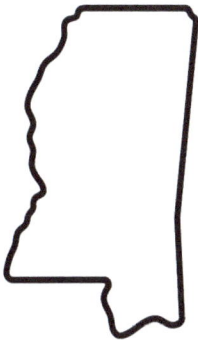
Mississippi

Tennessee

Georgia

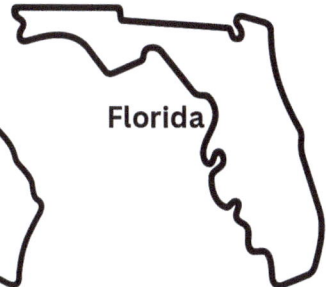
Florida

7

Montgomery, a city located in the state of Alabama, officially became the capital in 1846.

Montgomery, Alabama, has
an estimated population of
around 196,986 people.

State House
600 Dexter Avenue
Montgomery, Alabama 36104

Alabama, the 30th largest state in the United States, is often described as being of medium size in comparison to other states.

There are about 5,024,279 people who live in Alabama.

Huntsville, Alabama

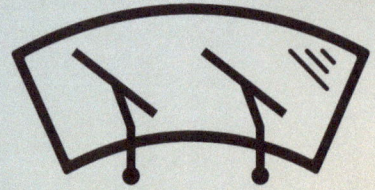

Mary Elizabeth Anderson, a native of Greene County, Alabama, is credited with inventing the first operational windshield wiper.

12

Lonnie George Johnson, a renowned inventor, was born in Mobile, Alabama. He is widely celebrated for inventing the iconic Super Soaker water gun.

Alabama

There are 67 counties in Alabama.

Here is a list of 20 of those counties:

Autauga	Chilton	Crenshaw	Jefferson
Barbour	Clarke	Cullman	Lawrence
Blount	Cleburne	Dale	Mobile
Butler	Colbert	Etowah	Russell
Chambers	Coosa	Greene	Walker

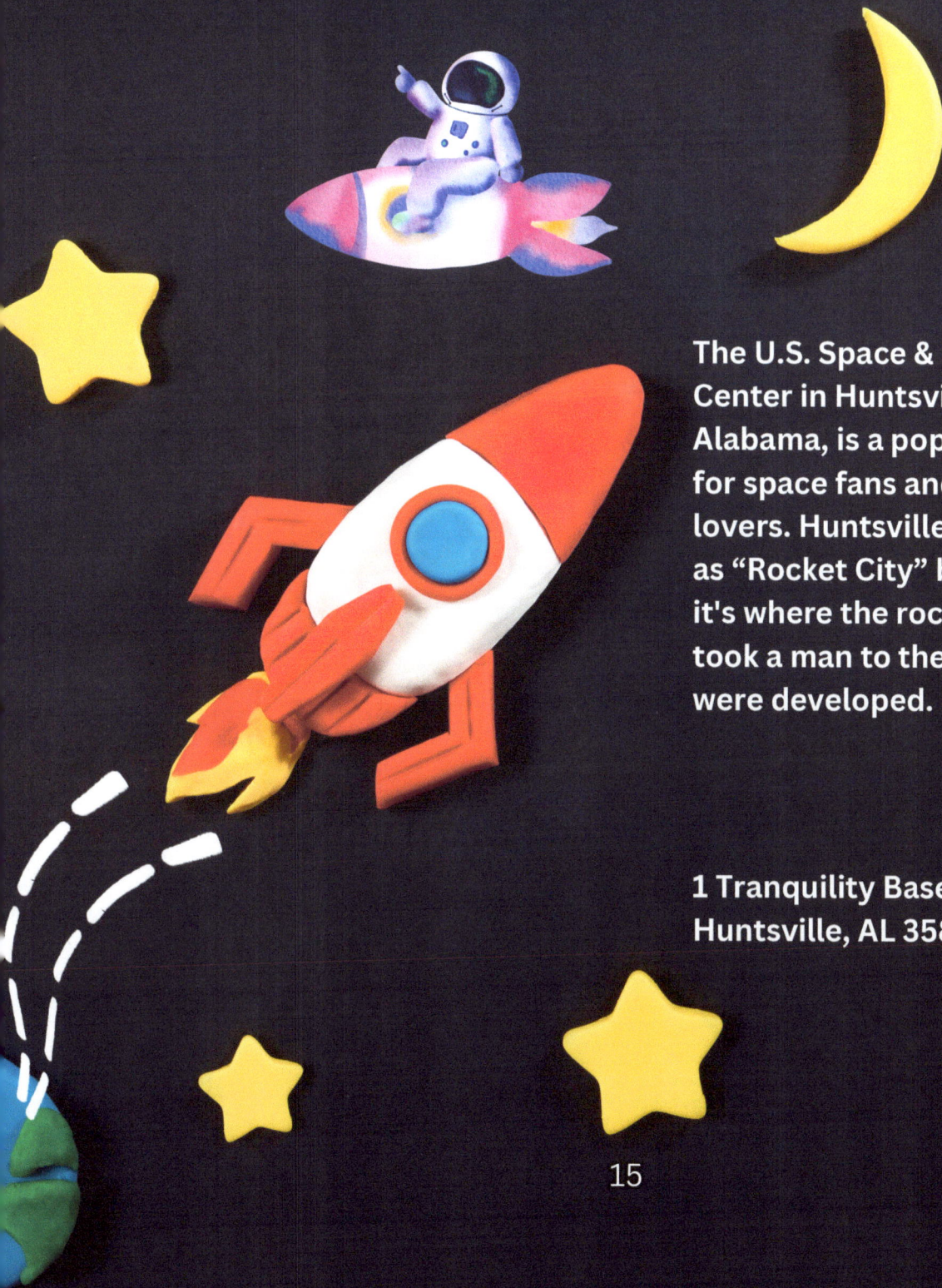

The U.S. Space & Rocket Center in Huntsville, Alabama, is a popular spot for space fans and history lovers. Huntsville is known as "Rocket City" because it's where the rockets that took a man to the moon were developed.

1 Tranquility Base
Huntsville, AL 35805

ALABAMA

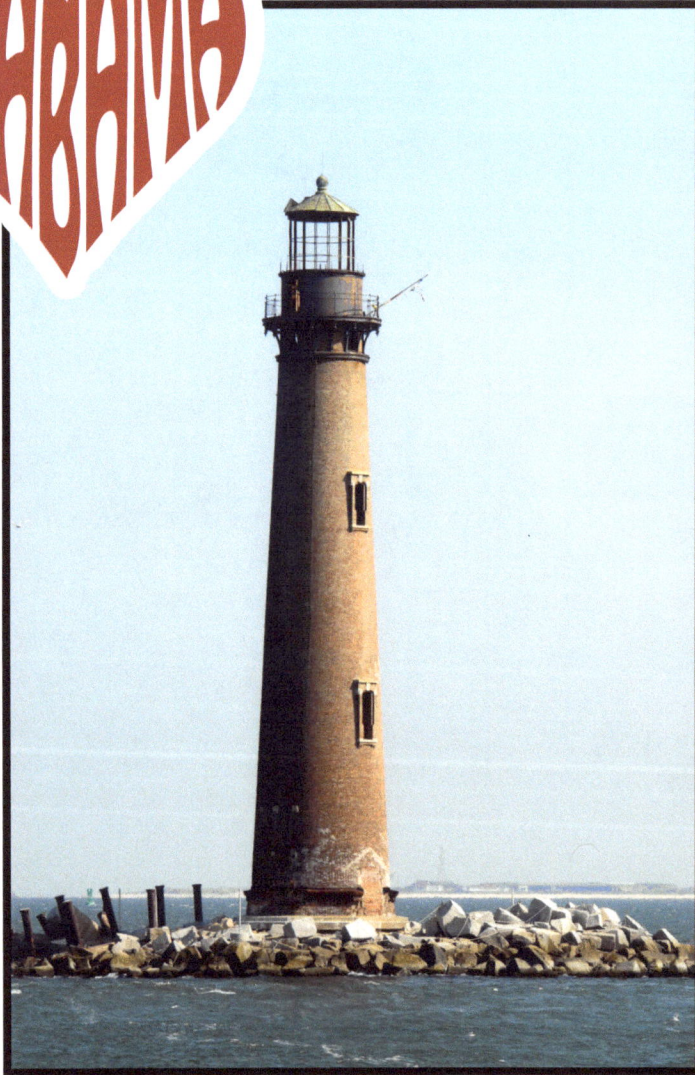

The Sand Island Lighthouse, also known as Sand Island Light, is situated near Dauphin Island at the entrance of Mobile Bay, Alabama.

In 1836, Alabama achieved a significant milestone by becoming the first state in the United States to formally acknowledge Christmas as an official holiday, marking a pivotal moment in American history.

Christmas

17

Mardi Gras

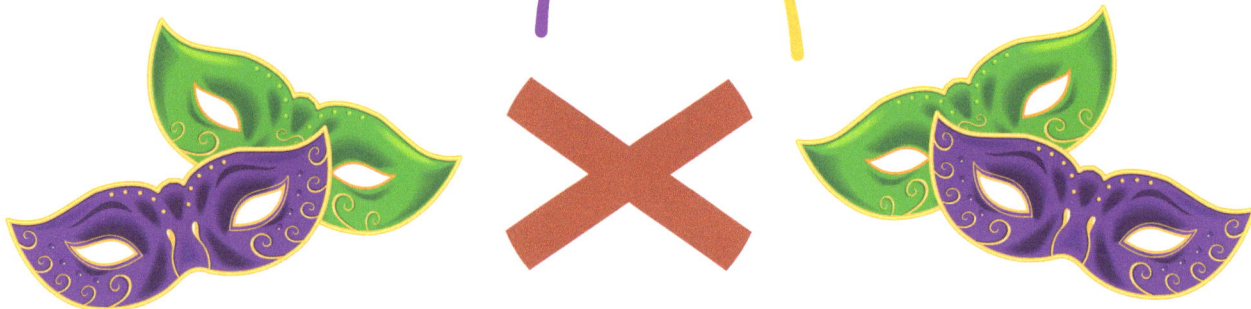

In 1703, the first Mardi Gras celebration in the United States was held in the vibrant city of Mobile, Alabama.

The official state bird of Alabama is the northern flicker, a beautiful woodpecker known for its striking yellow underwings and a rhythmic drumming sound as it pecks on trees. This bird is also commonly referred to as the Yellowhammer.

The Alabama official state flower is the Camellia. It became the state flower on April 18, 1918.

Fort Gaines, located on Dauphin Island in Mobile Bay, played a crucial role for the Confederate forces during the Civil War.

A few nicknames for Alabama include the Heart of Dixie, the Cotton State, and the Yellowhammer State.

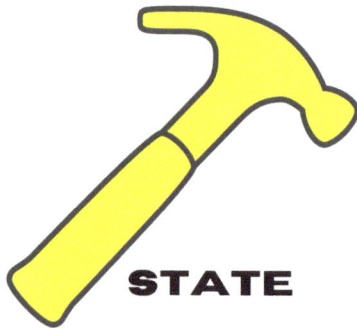
STATE

STATE

22

The Alabama state motto is "Audemus jura nostra defendere," which is a Latin phrase meaning "We Dare Defend Our Rights" The Alabama state motto was adopted in 1939.

1939

we ♡ DARE

ALABAMA
ALABAMA
ALABAMA
ALABAMA

The abbreviation for Alabama is AL.

AL

The Alabama state flag was adopted on February 16, 1895. It consists of a white background with a red diagonal cross, known as Saint Andrew's cross.

Some crops grown in Alabama are corn, cotton, grapes, peanuts, soybeans, and strawberries.

Some animals that inhabit Alabama include black bears, bobcats, groundhogs, deer, raccoons, squirrels, and skunks.

Alabama experiences extreme temperatures. The highest recorded was 112°F in Centreville on September 6, 1926, and the lowest was -27°F in New Market on January 30, 1966.

Hot

Cold

There is a unique distinction in the charming town of Magnolia Springs, Alabama: it is the only location in the United States with a year-round water mail delivery route, which started in 1915.

Oak Mountain State Park is a great place to visit. It is in Shelby County, AL.

**200 Terrace Drive
Pelham, AL 35124**

Some features of the park.

Fishing

Hiking

Basketball Court

Petting Zoo

Orange Beach is famous for its beautiful white sand beaches that stretch for miles along the coastline, creating a peaceful and picturesque setting. The area is great for families and welcomes travelers of all ages. The clear waters add to the beauty of this coastal paradise, offering a relaxing experience for visitors.

Orange Beach Welcome Center
23685 Perdido Beach Blvd.
Orange Beach, AL 36561

Water
Sports Hub

Ferris Wheel

Fishing

The University of Alabama's baseball team, known as the Alabama Crimson Tide, competes in NCAA Division I. They play their home games at Sewell–Thomas Stadium, a 6,571-seat baseball park located in Tuscaloosa, Alabama.

The Alabama State Hornets
football team represents
Alabama State University in
Montgomery, Alabama. They
are part of the NCAA FCS
Southwestern Athletic
Conference and play their
home games at The New ASU
Stadium in Montgomery.

In 1910, Wilbur and Orville Wright founded the nation's first civilian flying school in Montgomery, Alabama, marking a significant milestone in the history of aviation.

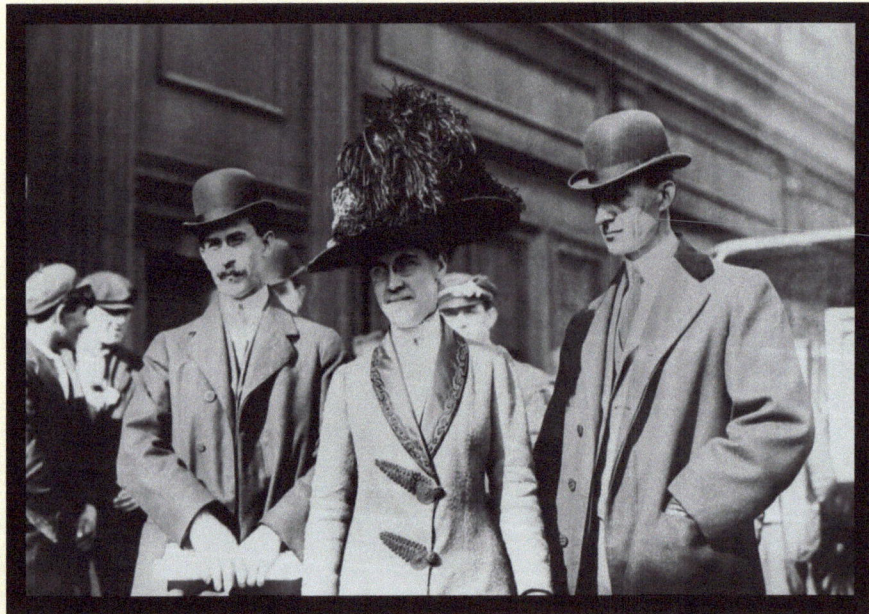

Orville, Katharine, and Wilbur Wright (siblings)

Can you name these?

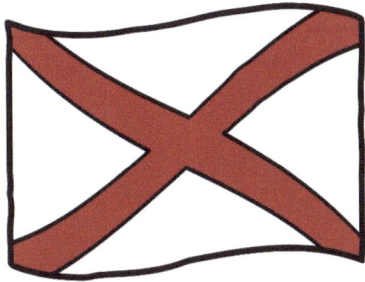

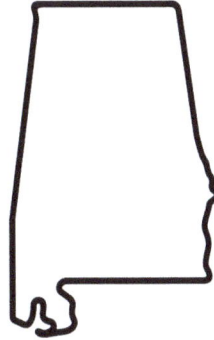

35

I hope you enjoyed
learning about
Alabama.

To explore fun facts about the other 49 states,
visit my website at www.joeysavestheday.com.
You'll also find a wide variety of homeschool
resources to support joyful learning at home.
If you enjoyed this book, I would be grateful if
you left a review. Your feedback truly helps.
Thank you for your support!

TIME
TO SAY
GOODBYE

Check out these other interesting books in the 50 States Fact Books Series!

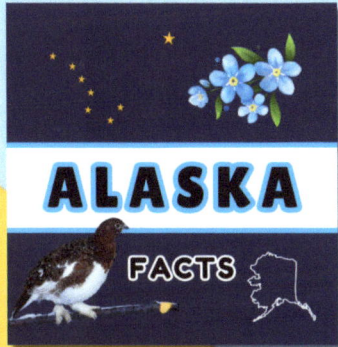

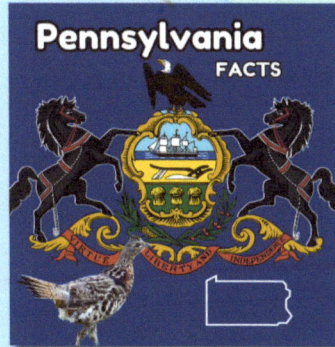

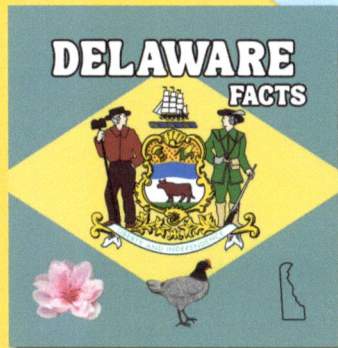

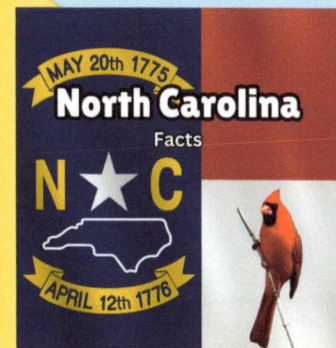

www.ingramcontent.com/pod-product-compliance
Lightning Source LLC
Chambersburg PA
CBHW041549040426
42447CB00002B/103